Novels for Students, Volume 58

Project Editor: Kristen A. Dorsch Rights Acquisition and Management: Ashley Maynard, Carissa Poweleit Composition: Evi Abou-El-Seoud

Manufacturing: Rita Wimberley

Imaging: John Watkins

For product information and technology assistance, contact us at **Gale Customer Support, 1-800-877-4253.**

For permission to use material from this text or product, submit all requests online at **www.cengage.com/permissions**.

Further permissions questions can be emailed to **permissionrequest@cengage.com** While every effort has been made to ensure the reliability of the information presented in this publication, Gale, A Cengage Company, does not guarantee the accuracy of the data contained herein. Gale accepts no payment for listing; and inclusion in the publication of any organization, agency, institution, publication, service, or individual does not imply endorsement of the editors or publisher. Errors brought to the attention of the publisher and verified to the satisfaction of the publisher will be corrected in future editions.

Gale
27500 Drake Rd.
Farmington Hills, MI, 48331-3535

ISBN-13: 978-1-4103-6557-6
ISSN 1094-3552

This title is also available as an e-book.
ISBN-13: 978-1-4103-9295-4
ISBN-10: 1-4103-9295-4
Contact your Gale, A Cengage Company sales

representative for ordering information.

Printed in Mexico
1 2 3 4 5 6 7 22 21 20 19 18

Passing

Nella Larsen

1929

Introduction

Nella Larsen's 1929 novel *Passing* questions the construction of race and gender in the United States through the story of Irene Redfield's reluctant friendship with Clare Kendry. Although both African American women easily pass as white, Clare has crossed over the color line to live in white society as the wife of a wealthy, racist international banker. When she is reunited with Irene, a childhood friend who enjoys a vibrant social life in Harlem, her desire to rejoin the African American community overpowers her own sense of self-preservation. Clare is the first to admit that she will do anything to get what she wants.

The novel complicates the familiar issues of race and gender identity through the unreliable narration of Irene, whose desire for economic security above all else is endangered by Clare's presence in her household. At once attracted to Clare and fearful that Clare is carrying on an affair with her dissatisfied husband, Brian, Irene sees Clare as a traitor of her race, gender, and class values yet feels compelled time and again to protect her. Only after Clare's white husband discovers the truth about his wife's race does Irene, sensing Clare's impending freedom, strike out against her.

Passing is a masterpiece of modern fiction that has inspired a plethora of critical interpretations. The novel's intricate web of contradictions and breathtaking dismissal of binary logic has led to Larsen's posthumous climb to the top of the ranks of Harlem Renaissance authors. In *Passing*, the division between white and black is exposed as a formative myth of the American people: as dangerous, false, and deadly as it is integral to the American way of life.

Author Biography

Larsen was born on April 13, 1891, in Chicago, Illinois, as Nella Walker. Her mother was Danish and her father West Indian. Her father died when Larsen was a young girl, and her mother remarried to a white man, leaving Larsen as the only dark-skinned member of her family. The facts of Larsen's biography are a subject of debate among scholars, and Larsen herself contributed a great deal to the confusion by frequently lying about her age, changing her name, and spreading false biographical information. Raised by her mother and stepfather in Denmark and the United States, she first attended Fisk Normal School in Nashville, Tennessee, where she studied science, followed by the University of Copenhagen.

She returned to the United States in 1912 to enroll at the Lincoln Hospital Training School for Nurses in New York City. She graduated in 1915, becoming the head nurse at Tuskegee Institute in Alabama. A year later, she returned to New York City to work for the Department of Health but found herself unsatisfied with a career in nursing. In 1919, she married Elmer Imes, the second black American in US history to earn a doctorate in physics. After accepting a position at the New York Public Library in 1921, Larsen began her writing career. Her short stories quickly won her the attention and support of well-known Harlem Renaissance authors and promoters such as Walter

White, W. E. B. Du Bois, and Carl Van Vechten.

Larsen's first novel, *Quicksand*, was published in 1928 and won Larsen wide praise. She was awarded the Harmon Foundation's Bronze Award for Literature, and a tea was hosted in her honor at the NAACP headquarters. Following this success, Larsen published *Passing* in 1929, once again delighting critics and readers with her ability to twist tropes and defy expectation swith her modernist prose. In 1930, Larsen was awarded a Guggenheim Fellowship on the strength and popularity of *Quicksand* and *Passing*. She traveled to Spain and France to conduct research for a third novel.

However, following the publication of her final short story, "Sanctuary," in 1930, Larsen was accused of plagiarism and fell from the height of her literary celebrity. In 1933, she divorced her husband following his infidelity with a colleague at Fisk University, where he worked as the head of the Physics Department. She vanished from the center of the Harlem Renaissance, working as a nurse at Bethel Hospital in Brooklyn. After retiring from the hospital in 1963, she died in obscurity in 1964. Her work was long overlooked until its rediscovery in the 1970s.

Plot Summary

Part One: Encounter

ONE

Irene Redfield receives a letter with no return address, but she knows it is from Clare Kendry. Reluctantly, she opens it. Clare begs her to meet her again, saying she has desperately longed to see her since they last met in Chicago. Irene blushes at Clare's words and at the memory of their last meeting. She remembers her anger and embarrassment and vows that she will not meet the catlike Clare again.

TWO

The scene shifts to two years previously, when Clare and Irene first met on a sweltering August day in Chicago. Irene is out shopping for her sons, Brian Jr. and Theodore, when, overcome by the heat, she realizes she might faint. She hails a cab and, telling the driver she needs tea and a cool breeze, he suggests the roof of the Drayton Hotel. There, Irene enjoys the peaceful atmosphere looking down at pedestrians below when a pretty woman and her companion arrive at the restaurant. The man leaves and the woman sits at a nearby table. She stares openly at Irene, making her self-conscious.

Irene wonders if, somehow, this woman can tell that Irene is African American, passing for white to enjoy the whites-only Drayton. She dismisses the idea: "Absurd! Impossible! White people were so stupid about such things for all that they usually asserted that they were able to tell." Still, Irene is paranoid, not wishing to be escorted from the Drayton for being African American. The woman approaches Irene. She recognizes her, calling her by a childhood nickname, but Irene does not remember knowing a pretty white woman. When Irene admits she does not know her, the woman laughs, and Irene realizes she is Clare Kendry.

No one has seen Clare for twelve years, though she has been spotted in the company of wealthy whites. Unlike Irene, who passes as white only occasionally, when it is convenient, Clare lives as a white person, concealing her true identity from everyone. Clare admits she has thought of Irene often, though Irene had forgotten about Clare. Clare begs Irene to come to dinner, but Irene has plans. Clare asks her to tea the next day, but Irene tells her no.

Clare wonders why more light-skinned black women do not pass permanently—she finds it so effortless. She was raised by two strict white great-aunts whom she ran away from at the age of eighteen to marry her husband, John Bellew. Irene tells her she would never pass full time, she finds her life satisfying as it is. Admiring Clare's beauty —her golden hair and dark eyes, Irene promises to try to visit her on Tuesday. However, once back on the street she feels resentment toward Clare, especially after she realizes Clare has failed to mention her new last name, leaving Irene with no way to find her again. She decides that she is through with Clare.

THREE

On Tuesday, Irene remains determined to avoid Clare, but Clare makes it impossible. The phone rings off the hook for hours until Irene at last gives in and answers Clare's call. She arrives for tea at Clare's apartment, where their mutual acquaintance, Gertrude Martin, is lounging on a sofa. Gertrude, too, can pass for white. She is married to a white man who knows that she is African American. Irene dislikes Gertrude and notices that she is not comfortable during their tea, waiting for Clare's husband to arrive. Clare tells them about her travels in Europe. Then they discuss their children. Gertrude has twin boys, and Clare has a daughter who attends boarding school in Europe.

Clare was paralyzed with the fear throughout her pregnancy that she might give birth to a darkskinned child. She is grateful Margery is light-skinned like her. Even though her husband did not care, Gertrude was terrified as well: "Why, he actually said he didn't care what colour it turned out, if I would only stop worrying about it. But, of course, nobody wants a dark child." Irene tells her that one of her sons is darkskinned. Gertrude recoils in embarrassment, asking awkwardly if Irene's husband is darkskinned, too. He is, Irene replies.

Clare tells Irene that only race traitors like her worry about such things and changes the subject.

Her husband, John, arrives. Irene notices at once that he is not the man she saw Clare with on the roof of the Drayton. He is a powerfully built but physically unremarkable man. He greets his wife: "Hello, Nig." Irene and Gertrude exchange a shocked glance. John explains with a good-humored laugh that every year he has been married to Clare she has gotten darker, thus the nickname.

Everyone laughs, but once Irene starts laughing she cannot stop, until she is crying. The others stare at her, bewildered. Clare asks John what would happen if he found out she was one or two percent African American. He tells her not to worry, she can get as dark as she likes because he knows she is not African American. There will never be any African Americans in his family, he assures the room. Irene asks if he dislikes African Americans. John tells her he does not dislike them: he hates them. Irene struggles to contain her anger. She asks if he has ever known an African American. He has not, but he has learned from the news that they are criminals. Irene fights the urge to shout that he is surrounded by three black women. Instead, she continues the conversation amiably. She admits that her husband is a successful doctor in New York City, but he wants to move to South America.

Irene leaves as soon as she can do so politely, seething with anger and burning with shame. Gertrude leaves with her and on the street bursts out with surprise at how crazy Clare must be to deceive such a racist man. Neither woman can believe that Clare did not see fit to warn them in advance. Clare's actions seem wildly reckless to both Gertrude and Irene, though Irene attempts to play down her shock. The women part ways. Alone with her anger, Irene cannot sleep that night. She decides not to worry about Clare. She can take care of herself. Any discomfort Irene feels is her own fault for going to the tea at all.

FOUR

The next morning as she is preparing to leave for New York, Irene receives a letter from Clare. After swearing she will not read it, Irene gives in immediately. Clare thanks her for visiting and hopes Irene will forgive her. She adds in a postscript that she is starting to think Irene's way of living might be wiser than passing. Irene is indignant. She tears the letter into small pieces and drops them over the railing of her room, watching the pieces flutter down. She swears she will never see Clare again. She thinks instead of her family in New York, especially her husband, Brian, who has recently grown distant and restless.

Part Two: Re-encounter

ONE

Sitting with Clare's second letter in her home in New York City, Irene vows not to see Clare again: "The trouble with Clare was, not only that she wanted to have her cake and eat it too, but that she wanted to nibble at the cakes of other folk as well." Irene debates with herself, wondering if she has a duty to Clare because of their shared race, even if Clare has no loyalty toward it. Brian enters the room. Irene lets him read Clare's letter. He asks if she will see Clare and warns her that Clare will pester her if given the opportunity. They discuss the attitudes of African American people toward passing. Their interactions are cold and sarcastic. They avoid the topic of Brazil, where Brian desperately wants to move. Irene refuses to consider it, resenting the fact that he will not let the subject drop. She wants Brian to be happy, but on her own terms.

TWO

Irene does not write Clare back, throwing her letter in the trash instead. After a week, Clare comes to visit unannounced. As soon as Irene sees her, she forgets her objections, exclaiming on Clare's beauty. Clare tells Irene she waited desperately for an answer to her letter. Irene tells her she does not think it is smart for Clare to socialize with African Americans, considering her husband's racism. Clare laughs at Irene's insistence that she be safe. She does not care. Even the threat of her daughter's safety does not hamper her determination to return to the African American community she left as a girl.

They are interrupted by a phone call. Hugh Wentworth, a famous author, is calling Irene with last-minute preparations for the Negro Welfare

League dance tomorrow. Hugh is white, but Irene explains that much of their social world in Harlem is mixed. Clare wants to attend the dance, though Irene has reservations. Clare insists: "You don't know, you can't realize how I want to see Negroes, to be with them again, to talk with them, to hear them laugh." Irene relents, officially inviting Clare along. After Clare leaves, however, Irene is angry with herself for giving in to Clare's demands.

THREE

Brian, Clare, and Irene attend the dance. Irene is pleased to see Brian and Clare getting along, hoping Clare will understand that black men are just as good as white men. Hugh asks Irene who the beautiful blonde woman is, and Irene explains that she is a childhood friend and an African American, too. He is stunned, proclaiming that every time he thinks he can tell he ends up wrong. Irene reassures him that no one can tell by looking: "I'm afraid I can't explain. Not clearly. There are ways. But they're not definite or tangible." Although African American people easily pass as white, white people cannot pass as African American, Irene argues. They would be discovered. At the end of the night Brian takes Clare home while Irene rides home with Bianca Wentworth, Hugh's wife. The night fades from Irene's mind, blurring with the memories of other dances.

FOUR

The dance would prove important as the start of Irene's friendship with Clare. Clare becomes a fixture at the Redfield house. Although Irene is partially pleased and somewhat annoyed by her visits, Brian seems amused. The children like Clare, and she becomes friends with the maids, much to Irene's embarrassment. Irene asks Brian if he thinks Clare is beautiful, and he answers no right away. He says she is pretty for a white woman, but he likes darker women. Clare and Brian attend parties together when Irene is unable to go. Irene's friends like Clare, who always seems a little distant and mysterious. Gradually, the threat of Clare's discovery by John fades from the forefront of Irene's mind. One day, Clare tells Irene how grateful she is for her friendship and apologizes for her own selfishness. She admits that she will do anything and hurt anyone to get what she wants. Suddenly, she starts to cry.

Part Three: Finale

ONE

Brian's discontent grows. Irene wonders if his longing for Brazil is truly the cause. He wakes her up from a nap before a party for Hugh to tell her Clare has arrived. Irene says she did not invite Clare because she senses that Hugh is not fond of her. Brian sheepishly admits that he was the one to invite her, apologizing for his misstep. All at once Irene suspects that Brian and Clare are having an affair. When Brian leaves to attend to Clare and the other guests, Irene bursts into tears. She collects herself and goes downstairs to tea. While Irene mingles with her guests, Clare and Brian sit talking. Hugh, too, notices them together. Irene's suppressed rage builds, and she drops her teacup. It shatters. She tells Hugh she dropped it on purpose, because she hated the design. Irene clings to the thought of her boys in order to survive the devastation she feels inside.

TWO

Irene attempts to convince herself that the affair is not real but a figment of her imagination. She has no proof of her suspicions. However, she is tired of Clare's company and cannot wait until March, when she will sail to Europe with John: "If something would only happen, something that would make John Bellew decide on an earlier departure, or that would remove Clare. Anything. She didn't care what." Irene considers telling John the truth about his wife.

THREE

The very next day, Irene runs into John on Fifty-seventh Street. He doffs his hat to her, but his smile fades when he sees that Irene is arm and arm with her friend, Felise Freeland, who is obviously African American. John looks between them, something like understanding on his face. He holds out his hand, but Irene does not take it. She passes by without a word, wasting her opportunity to tell John about Clare. She feels obligated to warn Clare about the incident but decides it is too late. She may be rid of her for good. She does not tell Brian, either. Irene realizes that if John were to divorce

Clare, Clare would be utterly free. Irene cannot have that. She wishes Clare would die but recoils from the thought: "Above everything else she had wanted, had striven, to keep undisturbed the pleasant routine of her life. And now Clare Kendry had come into it, and with her the menace of impermanence."

FOUR

The next morning, there is a snowstorm, but Clare calls to tell Irene she can make it to the party at Felise's that night. At dinner, Brian attempts to explain racism to his sons, but Irene will not allow it. Brian does not understand why Irene wants to live in a country with rampant racism but believes she can keep her sons from experiencing it. If it were up to him, they would not live in the United States. Clare arrives while Irene is getting ready. Irene shrinks from her kisses, though Clare does not notice. Irene asks if she has really considered what would happen if her husband found her out. Clare says yes and smiles. Her smile fills Irene with dread. Clare admits that if John divorced her, she could come live in Harlem and do as she pleases.

Irene tells Clare to go downstairs and wait with Brian while she finishes getting ready. She tells herself that the affair is real and is surprised to discover she is numb toward the fact. She longs for security, questioning if she has ever truly known love. Whether or not she loves Brian, she feels that it is his duty to be beside her. She will not let him go. That night Clare, Brian, and Irene arrive at

Felise's sixth-floor apartment. Irene holds one of Brian's arms while Clare holds the other, but Brian's attention remains on Clare alone.

The party begins. Only Irene sits apart from the warm social atmosphere. She opens a window to cool off and drops her cigarette out, watching it fall the long distance to the ground. Suddenly the doorbell rings, and John pushes into the room, shouting that he knows his wife is there. He finds Clare, shouting that he knows she is African American and lied to him. Clare stands by the window, her face perfectly calm. Irene is enraged by her composure and rushes across the room to put her hand on Clare: "What happened next, Irene Redfield never afterwards allowed herself to remember. Never clearly. One moment Clare had been there…. The next she was gone." John gasps and calls after his wife in agony, using his crude nickname for her. The party rushes downstairs, but Irene stays behind.

Irene is not sorry that Clare is gone. She only wonders what the others will think. The thought of Brian downstairs in the cold without a coat moves her to leave the apartment. She worries over how to explain why she remained behind. She worries, too, that Clare survived the fall. She finds the others gathered around Clare's body. They assumed Irene fainted and tell her that Clare died instantly. An authority figure asks Irene if Clare fell or if her husband pushed her. Irene tells them she fell. Her knees give out, and "then everything was dark."

Characters

Authority Figure

The authority figure is a vague voice Irene hears in the confusion following Clare's death. The voice asks if Irene saw whether Clare fell or was pushed from the window.

Clare Kendry Bellew

Clare is a childhood friend of Irene's. They grew up together in Chicago until Clare's father died when she was fifteen and Clare went to live with her white aunts. After discovering her ability to pass, Clare married John at the age of eighteen and began to live as a white woman. She has a daughter, Margery, who attends boarding school in Switzerland. Her husband travels constantly for work, leaving Clare alone. Irene first sees her at the Drayton Hotel in the company of a man who is not her husband. She suspects that Clare is unfaithful to John.

Clare, conscious of her racial deception, refuses to hire African American servants and invites only her friends who are light enough to pass to the tea she hosts in Chicago. However, Clare is desperate for the company of African Americans and insists on making friends with a reluctant Irene to achieve this goal while living temporarily in New

York City. Clare so enjoys her time with Irene that she wishes she could escape her marriage entirely. She tells Irene she considers motherhood a curse and knows that she would be free if John discovered her race. While Irene is certain that Clare is carrying on an affair with Brian, there is no direct evidence, though it is true the two are frequently alone together.

Clare's behavior towards Irene is excessively friendly, and the intimate tone of her letters makes Irene blush. She calls Irene "'Rene," a childhood nickname. Clare dies after falling from the window of Felise's apartment, but Irene does not state explicitly whether she was pushed, by either Irene or John, or she jumped.

Clare Kendry Bellew's Aunts

Clare's aunts, Edna and Grace, are actually her great-aunts, both of whom are white. They are very religious old women who raised Clare. They believe African Americans are inherently lazy and made Clare work nonstop as a girl. Clare ran away from their home when she turned eighteen to marry John.

Clare Kendry Bellew's Companion

When Irene first sees Clare on the roof of the Drayton Hotel, she is with a male companion. The two seem intimately familiar, and the man leaves Clare after they exchange warm goodbyes. Irene is later shocked to discover that Clare's companion is not her husband.

Jack Bellew

See John Bellew

John Bellew

John grew up near Clare's aunts. She met him after he had just returned from South America with gold. Clare calls John by her nickname for him, Jack. Clare ran away from home to marry John when she turned eighteen. John travels abroad frequently as an international banking agent. He is openly racist, calling his wife by his nickname for her, "Nig," because of her darkening complexion. He cheerfully tells Irene at the tea party that he has never known an African American personally, but he is sure he hates them. He has read in the news how they are violent criminals. John first seems to suspect the truth about Clare after he sees Irene out shopping with Felise. He demands entry into the Freelands' party at the end of the novel to confront Clare about her race. After Irene rushes to Clare and Clare falls out the window, John cries out in pain: "There was a gasp of horror, and above it a sound not quite human, like a beast in agony." John disappears from the scene of his wife's death.

Margery Bellew

Margery is the daughter of Clare and John. She attends a boarding school in Switzerland. Clare isnot particularly attentive to or interested in her daughter's life.

Cab Driver

The cab driver who picks Irene up in Chicago suggests that she can escape the heat at the Drayton Hotel. He mistakes her for a white woman.

Dave Freeland

Dave Freeland is Felise's husband. He tries in vain to cheer Irene up at his party.

Felise Freeland

Felise Freeland is Irene's friend. Unlike Irene, she is obviously African American, and when John sees the two women together he seems to understand that Irene is African American as well. Felise is carefree and likes to joke. She hosts the party in the final scene along with her husband, Dave.

Bob Kendry

Bob Kendry was Clare's father. He worked as a janitor until he was killed in a saloon fight when Clare was fifteen years old. His face is described as "pasty-white."

Junior

See Brian Redfield Jr.

Fred Martin

Fred is Gertrude's white husband. He knows that Gertrude is African American, but he does not care. He also does not care if their children are dark-skinned.

Gertrude Martin

Gertrude attends the tea in Chicago with Irene, Clare, and John. Gertrude married a white man, but unlike John, Gertrude's husband is aware of her race. Gertrude is light-skinned enough to pass as white. Irene finds her to be coarse, and her animosity grows after Gertrude states that no one wants dark-skinned children. After Gertrude and Irene escape the awkward tea together, Gertrude calls Clare crazy for deceiving such an openly racist man.

Gertrude Martin's Twin Boys

Gertrude's twin boys are light-skinned. Gertrude was terrified of having dark-skinned children, but her husband, Fred, did not care about their skin color.

Brian Redfield

Brian is Irene's husband and the father of Theodore and Brian Jr. He is dark-skinned and handsome. He works as a doctor in Manhattan but longs to move to Brazil, where racial divisions are more fluid. Irene refuses to consider the idea, making it a sore topic in their marriage. Brian is restless and distant, and his conversation is marked by his dry sense of humor. He is nice to Clare, to Irene's surprise, and she soon suspects an affair between them. After Brian invites Clare to a party in Hugh's honor without consulting Irene, she feels her suspicions are confirmed. The two seem especially close the night of the Freelands' party, and Brian is devastated by Clare's death. As a father, Brian advocates for honesty and openness with his sons, even when discussing difficult topics such as racism. Irene opposes this open attitude, feeling the children should be sheltered from such truths until they are older.

Brian Redfield Jr.

Brian Jr. is Clare and Brian's older son.

Irene Westover Redfield

Irene is the novel's narrator. Her life is changed when she is reunited with along-lost childhood friend, Clare. Irene is light-skinned and capable of passing, but she does so only when it is convenient. For example, she chooses to pass only twice in the novel: at the Drayton and at Clare's tea. Otherwise, Irene lives as an African American woman, married to a dark-skinned man. She is active in the African American community of Harlem, organizing and attending dances, parties, and teas.

As the wife of a doctor, Irene belongs to the African American upper middle class. She does not socialize with the lower class and finds Clare's friendship with her maids childish and inappropriate. Clare both disturbs and fascinates Irene. Although she states several times that she will not see her again, Irene continues to extend invitations to Clare. Irene especially admires Clare's beauty, often forgiving Clare for slights and transgressions she has built up in her mind when she sees Clare in person. Though she struggles with her friendship with Clare, Irene has countless other friends, including the famous author Hugh Wentworth.

Irene believes in racial uplift and works toward that goal through her charitable works. She will not move to Brazil and hates discussing the topic with Brian, causing a rift between them. Irene is an unreliable narrator who often justifies her behavior in moralistic terms, considering herself inherently superior to Clare because she is not a race traitor. The truth is more complicated, as Irene harbors several racist instincts and is the victim of her own sexual repression. Just as Clare looks white but is in truth African American, Irene says all the right things about racial issues but struggles to connect with her own people.

'Rene Redfield

See Irene Redfield

Theodore Redfield

Theodore Redfield is Clare and Brian's younger son.

Sadie

Sadie is one of Irene's maids. Irene finds Clare's habit of chatting with Sadie embarrassing.

Waiter

The waiter works at the rooftop restaurant where Clare and Irene meet. Irene finds the flirtatious way Clare looks at the waiter to be overbold and inappropriate.

Bianca Wentworth

Bianca Wentworth is Hugh's wife. She gives Irene a ride home after the Negro Welfare League dance.

Hugh Wentworth

Hugh is Irene's dear friend, a famous white author who socializes with the African American community in Harlem. Hugh has an animated discussion with Irene about race at the Negro Welfare League dance, where he admits he cannot tell that Clare is African American.

Zulena

Zulena is one of Irene's maids. Irene refers to her as a "mahogany-colored creature." Irene considers Clare's friendly behavior toward Zulena to be inappropriate.

Themes

Race Relations

In *Passing*, the ability of African Americans to pass as white erodes the perceived division between races. While in the United States, especially in the 1920s, the races were strictly defined with no official movement possible between them, in Brazil, where Brian longs to move, there are a multitude of races, and the divisions between them are fluid. This is closer to the reality of the spectrum of human skin tones than the American insistence on binary opposition. If Clare looks white, what, exactly, makes her African American and thus unequal to her husband? The novel does not answer the question because there is no rational explanation. If skin tone does not denote race, is it the community and culture in which one belongs? Again, the answer is nebulous.

Topics for Further Study

- Read a poem, short story, play, or novel by another Harlem Renaissance writer. Create a PowerPoint presentation about that writer's life and work, including a biography, list of works, relevant photos, reviews, and an excerpt and explication of the work you read. Your presentation should have a minimum of ten slides as well as a works-cited slide. Authors and poets to choose from include Langston Hughes, Zora Neale Hurston, Jean Toomer, Jessie Fauset, James Weldon Johnson, Dorothy West, Jacob Johnson, Augusta Savage, Claude McKay, and many more.

- In small groups, discuss the

characterization of Clare Kendry. Is she sympathetic in the novel or a villain? What are her motivations? How does she feel toward Irene? What are her opinions about passing? What do you think is the cause of Clare's fall from the window at the end of the novel, and why? How would the novel change if Clare were the narrator instead of Irene? Take notes with your group and hold a class discussion.

- Using print and online resources, research to learn more about the case of Rachel Dolezal. Why did Dolezal choose to pass as black? What were the consequences of being caught passing? What arguments have been made for and against her right to assume the identity of an African American woman? What racial issues raised in *Passing* can you apply to Dolezal? Write an essay in which you compare Clare Kendry's passing to Dolezal's. In what ways does the discussion of race change when discussing a white person passing as African American rather than an African American person passing as white, and why? Include a works-cited page at the end of your essay.

- Read Sherri L. Smith's young-adult novel *Flygirl* (2010). What are the risks and rewards for passing for Ida Mae? What role does gender play in the novel? How do those who do not pass—both white and African American—react toward Ida Mae's decision to pass? Write an essay in which you briefly summarize the novel and answer these questions.

Clare lives in white society for twelve years but is still considered African American, while Irene's Harlem is so popular with whites that Brian jokes one day soon African Americans will not be allowed inside their own venues. If race is determined by ancestry, such as the onedrop rule that was prevalent in the United States, who is responsible for keeping those who appear white but have a single African American ancestor neatly separated from white society? The liminal space between white and African American defies discriminatory laws and racial stereotypes. John Bellew tells the three African American women having a tea party in his home that all African Americans are violent criminals, while Clare and Irene are strictly forbidden from dining on the roof of the Drayton. However, for such high stakes, passing is easy for these middle-class women, making a mockery of the American obsession with racial purity and hierarchy. Race crumbles from reality to fantasy in *Passing*. The divisions are a sinister invention, not a fact.

Sexuality

Irene's repressed sexuality leads to her suspicion of an affair between Brian and Clare. Irene finds sex to be an inappropriate subject and one that is difficult to discuss. Her relationship with her husband reflects this attitude: they sleep in separate bedrooms and speak to each other with ironic humor and chilly sarcasm rather than with romance or gentleness. Clare's flirtatious nature is a sharp contrast to Irene's chilly disposition.

Irene finds Clare's upward gazing stare to be too bold, especially after she discovers that Clare is African American. In Irene's mind, women should be mothers first, and under no circumstances should they be the aggressor in pursuing a mate. Clare first appears in the flesh in the novel with a man who is not her husband. She proceeds to flirt with the waiter on the roof of the Drayton Hotel. Her profoundly intimate letter makes Irene blush. Irene is surprised at first that Brian is kind to Clare and soon suspects an affair between them.

Irene sees Clare's actions as inappropriate in part because Clare defies Irene's strict ideas about gender roles in her aggressive pursuit of romance. She is uninterested in her role as a mother and refuses to remain passive in the face of what she wants. Clare even admits she will do anything to get the object of her desire. The tension between Clare and Irene is the result of Irene's own attraction to

Clare. Irene admires her constantly, finding her beauty impossible to ignore. So powerful is Irene's latent attraction that she assumes everyone in her orbit admires Clare just as much. Though Brian states plainly he does not find Clare attractive and despite the fact that he has never strayed from Irene's side, Irene presumes he is having an affair with Clare, projecting her own forbidden desires. Whether the affair is a reality or a figment of Irene's imagination, Clare's sexuality is a direct threat to Irene's security.

Wealth

Irene's most precious commodity is her affluent middle-class lifestyle, afforded to her by her marriage to a prominent Manhattan doctor. Her financial security and social status represent Irene's greatest interests. She may not admit it as easily as Clare, but Irene will do whatever it takes to protect her lifestyle. She employs two maids, attends teas, dances, and parties, dresses in fine clothes, and wonders if she should send her sons to be educated in Europe in order to escape the crudeness of American children. For these luxuries, Irene is willing to remain in an increasingly loveless marriage and works against the current of her husband and sons' wishes to control her household's image.

Clare, too, is fantastically wealthy, having married rich. However, she seems to care nothing for her economic security, eagerly risking it all simply to socialize with members of her own race. To status-conscious Irene, this dismissal of economic security is outrageously offensive. Clare rejects not only the security itself but also the values associated with such social status. She cheats on her husband, regrets having her daughter, and longs to climb down, not up, the social ladder, from the wealthy white world to the upper-middle-class African American society where Irene makes her home.

Though Irene organizes a dance for the Negro Welfare League, she has no interest in impoverished blacks. Her race consciousness—a point of personal pride—is heavily influenced by her class, as well as the ideals of white high society: if her life of endless small talk at a neverending blur of parties seems empty and unfulfilling, at least she is not a "creature" like her dark-skinned, lower-class maid, Zulena. Irene is bound by a fear of losing her status and thus cannot move freely, as Clare does. Before Irene can act, she must consider appearances. When she finally snaps, her primary concern is not abject horror at what she has done but paralyzing fear of what her peers will think of her.

Foil

A foil in a work of literature is a character whose appearance, behavior, or personality traits are in opposition to the protagonist's. By comparing the protagonist to a foil, readers reach a deeper understanding of the protagonist's nature. In *Passing*, Clare and Irene are each other's foils. Each woman is exposed and defined by her difference from the other. For example, Clare lives in white society, whereas Irene lives in African American society, although both are African American and both can pass as white with little effort. Clare and Irene are both locked in marriages characterized by misunderstanding, but Clare yearns to escape, whereas Irene clings to her family. Likewise, Clare has no interest in the life of her daughter, whereas Irene defines herself as a mother. Clare is openly flirtatious and may be exploring extramarital affairs, whereas Irene represses her sexuality and finds discussions of the topic inappropriate. These contrasts between the two women provide a deeper understanding of their attitudes toward race, gender, and class. The tension between the two foils in *Passing* creates the narrative complexity that has transfixed readers for decades.

Unreliable Narrator

In a work of fiction, an unreliable narrator is a narrator who—whether consciously or unconsciously—attempts to deceive the reader. Irene Redfield is an example of an unreliable narrator, whose words cannot be trusted at face value. Though the narration in this case is not from a first-person point of view, the novel is told through the limited third person and follows her thoughts closely. She often justifies her actions in terms of her loyalty to the African American race, her altruism, or her love of her family. In fact, Irene's views toward race are problematic and, at times, blatantly racist. She refers to her maid Zulena as a "mahogany-colored creature," dehumanizing her and remarking on her skin tone in the same breath. Irene's charitable work is done out of a need for social recognition rather than a true desire to help others. The plight of poor African Americans rarely enters Irene's mind, whereas her social status is of utmost concern. Likewise, her family is a symbol of her stability and success. She attempts to control them and the image they project, rather than nurturing them as a truly devoted mother and wife would. Clare's presence in Irene's life triggers layers of denial—of her sexuality, racism, and class-conscious lifestyle. According to Irene, Clare is the traitor and liar, not Irene. Clare is selfish and cruel, not Irene. Yet Clare easily admits her faults, while Irene attempts always to convince the reader of her moral high ground.

The Harlem Renaissance

The Harlem Renaissance was a period of prolific artistic, intellectual, and social activity in the traditionally African American New York City neighborhood of Harlem from 1917 to 1935. Along with Larsen, authors and poets associated with the Harlem Renaissance include Langston Hughes, Zora Neale Hurston, Jean Toomer, Arna Bontemps, Walter White, and many more. Those immersed in the movement encouraged African Americans to move to Harlem to take part in the cultural upheaval, especially those living in the Jim Crow–era southern United States, where oppression and intolerance were rampant. Although Jim Crow laws were in place in the northern states as well—illustrated in *Passing* by the Drayton Hotel—many whites were attracted to the activity in Harlem and openly attended events there. Larsen disappeared from the Harlem Renaissance social scene shortly before its demise, caused in part by the onset of the Great Depression.

Compare & Contrast

- **1929:** Though women earn the right to vote in 1919, a decade later the inequality between genders remains profound. Men are considered the head of the household and primary breadwinner, while women are confined to the roles of mother and homemaker, though many find work outside their homes in careers such as nursing and teaching—jobs considered suitable for their gender.

Today: Although women have joined the workforce in larger numbers each year since World War II, they remain the victims of institutionalized sexism and misogyny. Women make 83 percent of what their male counterparts earn, but the wage gap continues to narrow thanks to the efforts of feminist activists.

- **1929:** Racial discrimination is a fact of life, with discriminatory laws—called Jim Crow laws—in place across the United States ensuring the unequal treatment of African Americans in all walks of life.

  Today: By law, it is illegal to discriminate against people based on the color of their skin in the United States.

- **1929:** The American public is fascinated by the phenomenon of passing, with media outlets reporting on the prevalence of passers at a time when tensions between African Americans and whites are especially high.

Today: The case of Rachel Dolezal, in which the president of the Spokane, Washington, chapter of the NAACP was revealed to be a white woman passing for African American, draws national media coverage. Dolezal's insistence on the validity of her African American identity despite being born white sparks fierce debate over racism, white privilege, and the construction of race in the United States.

The Rhinelander Case

The Rhinelander case, which Irene mentions by name in the novel, was a famous trial in which a wealthy white man, Leonard Kip Rhinelander, sued his wife, Alice Beatrice Jones, for fraud. He claimed that he was unaware of her mixed race when he married her and that she had deliberately deceived him in order to gain access to his immense fortune. In truth, Leonard was quoted in a newspaper article shortly after their October 14, 1924, wedding, stating he did not care about Alice's race because they were deeply in love. It was Leonard's father who urged his son to annul the marriage, rejecting the introduction of African American blood into their family.

The trial, which began on November 9, 1925, was the subject of sensationalist news coverage, especially by papers with a predominantly white readership, whereas African American newspapers took a more sober tone. The most scandalous and degrading moment of the trial came when Alice was forced to show her almostnude body to the jury, judge, and lawyers. The jury was entirely white and male, and Alice wept while appearing before them naked from the waist up. This atrocious, dehumanizing treatment of Alice was meant to prove that the color of her skin was visible to her lover. In addition, Alice and Leonard's intimate love letters were read aloud to the courtroom in another breach of privacy, to the editorial delight of the newspapers covering the trial.

The jury did not find Alice guilty of fraud, handing down their verdict on December 5, 1925. Alice sued successfully for a separation in 1927, citing emotional damages after the Ku Klux Klan had threatened her life following the media frenzy surrounding the trial. She continued to sue both Leonard and his father with success until 1930, when their divorce was finalized. Alice agreed to a cash payment of $31,500 and an additional $3,600 every three months for the remainder of her life. The Rhinelander case in *Passing* works as an example of the high risk Clare runs by deceiving her wealthy husband, considering the humiliation Alice Beatrice Jones was subjected to while on trial, despite her innocence.

Critical Overview

Passing debuted to positive reviews upon its publication and was widely read, with critics praising Larsen's economical language and treatment of race. The year after its publication, Larsen became the first African American woman creative writer to be awarded a Guggenheim Fellowship. However, Larsen and her novels were long neglected following the end of the Harlem Renaissance.

Passing was rediscovered in the late twentieth century, when feminist critics and literary historians studying the Harlem Renaissance became aware of the complexities of meaning hidden within the novel's plot. A proliferation of critical analysis followed, with hundreds of essays written on the work. Josh Toth writes of critics' fascination with *Passing* in "Deauthenticating Community: The Passing Intrusion of Clare Kendry in Nella Larsen's *Passing*,"

> We might say that there is a critical tendency to approach *Passing* in the same way that Irene approaches Clare: as a type of mystery that must be solved, a dangerously unstable object that requires stabilization.

Margaret Gillespie examines the ways in which *Passing* overturns expectations of race and gender in "Gender, Race, and Space in Nella

Larsen's *Passing* (1929)":

> By taking the spatial image of
> passing as its central theme,
> metaphor and discursive modus
> operandi, Larsen's *Passing* engages
> with and troubles ...racial and
> gender binary paradigms and reveals
> as fraudulent... the stereotypes on
> which they are predicated.

Clare, especially, disrupts social conventions
and rejects the 1920s standards of feminine and
African American behavior. She stands in stark
contrast to Irene, who values the security of married
life, racial morality, and her role as a mother above
all else. Candice Jenkins writes in "Decoding
Essentialism: Cultural Authenticity and the Black
Bourgeoisie in Nella Larsen's *Passing*:" "In its
challenge to other characters' desire for lucid sexual
and racial boundaries, the body of the ambiguously
raced figure is ... an unsettled and unsettling
presence in the black bourgeois social sphere."
Clare occupies an always-shifting liminal space,
making her a natural enemy of those, like Irene,
who prefer certainty, order, and rules, especially in
their social interactions with others.

Though Irene lives as an African American
woman who passes for white only occasionally, she,
too, participates in the destruction of the concept of
race in the novel. It is because of her transgression
of the color line that she first encounters Clare in
Chicago, passing as white on the roof of the
Drayton Hotel. As Thadious M. Davis explains in

the introduction to the Penguin edition of the novel,

> Passing becomes a trope for representing black women of a particular physicality as transgressive subjects able to negotiate the ideologies compartmentalizing American life … to subvert the rigidity of color caste specifically and gender roles implicitly.

In "Introduction: Nella Larsen's Erotics of Race," Carla Kaplan examines the latent desire between Clare and Irene, a subject of intense scrutiny by modern critics that was overlooked at the time of the novel's original publication. "Through the growing attraction between Irene and Clare," Kaplan points out, "Larsen can depict characters who long for things they do not believe in and who believe in things which they find they do not want." On the forefront of the study of the attraction between Irene and Clare is Deborah E. McDowell, who writes in "Black Female Sexuality in *Passing*," "Although Irene is clearly deluded about her motives, her racial loyalty, her class, and her distinctness from Clare, the narrative suggests that her most glaring delusion concerns her feelings for Clare." McDowell suggests that, as an unreliable narrator, Irene cannot confront her desire for another woman, and so she projects her desire for Clare onto Brian instead. In this way, the affair between them that so disturbs Irene is an invention of her own mind as it protects itself from a dangerous, destabilizing sexual awakening.

Miriam Thaggert, in "Racial Etiquette: Nella Larsen's *Passing* and the Rhinelander Case," summarizes the ambiguities of the novel that have continued to enthrall readers and critics alike: "The reader never learns explicitly the reason for Clare's fall[,] ...the reality of a homosexual longing between Clare and Irene, or the true nature of the relationship between Clare and Irene's husband." Like the ambiguous Clare herself, the novel resists strict interpretation or categorization. It is a singularly unique work of art in its own time and in ours.

What Do I Read Next?

- In Jessie Fauset's *Plum Bun* (1928), Angela Murray moves to New York City to reinvent herself as a white woman after discovering that she can pass. Believing race to be the one thing holding her back from a happy and successful life, Angela soon learns that there are other factors keeping her from achieving her true potential.

- Larsen's *Quicksand* (1928) tells the story of Helga Crane, a mixed-race woman who searches the world for a place where she truly belongs. This epic story follows her journey across America and Europe's black and white communities, depicting the struggle of a woman with a mind of her own and a willingness to follow her heart wherever it leads.

- In Zora Neale Hurston's *Their Eyes Were Watching God* (1937), Janie Crawford shocks her small town when she shakes off the yoke of her powerful husband and opens her heart to a new and unexpected love. Janie's confident defiance of class and patriarchy has made her a timeless and beloved heroine of American literature.

- Alice Walker's *The Color Purple* (1982) was awarded the Pulitzer Prize and National Book Award for its depiction of one woman's struggle against poverty, abuse, racism, and rape. The lonely, broken Celie finds a friend in Shug, her violent husband's glamorous mistress, and the two women form an unforgettable bond that changes their lives forever.

- In Malorie Blackman's young-adult novel *Noughts and Crosses* (2006), two starcrossed lovers must overcome a strict racial divide. In an alternate universe, the lightskinned noughts are subject to the rule of the dark-skinned crosses, and no cross is more powerful than Sephy's father, the new prime minister. When Sephy's nought love, Callum, is suspected of a terrorist plot against the crosses, their happy, secret world crumbles as the truth is revealed.

- Edwidge Danticat's *The Farming of Bones* (1998) is based on the true story of the Parsley Massacre, in which the Dominican army, under the orders of the infamous dictator Rafael Trujillo, orders the slaughter of Haitian workers. So close are the Haitians and Dominicans in appearance that the soldiers used their pronunciation of the Spanish word for parsley to determine who will live and who will die. Protagonist Amabelle must run for her life to escape the massacre as it closes in on all sides, isolating her in a brutal world.

- *A Chosen Exile: A History of Racial Passing in America*, by Allyson Hobbs (2014), explores the history of blacks passing as whites in the United States with a particular focus on the risks and sacrifices those who pass must face as well as the advantages that draw passers to conceal their identities.

Sources

Davis, Thadious M., Introduction to *Passing*, Penguin Books, 2003, pp. vii–xxxii.

Gillespie, Margaret, "Gender, Race, and Space in Nella Larsen's *Passing* (1929)," in the *Journal of Research in Gender Studies*, Vol. 5, No. 2, July 1, 2015, pp. 279–89.

Jenkins, Candice M., "Decoding Essentialism: Cultural Authenticity and the Black Bourgeoisie in Nella Larsen's *Passing*," in *MELUS*, Vol. 30, No. 3, Fall 2005, pp. 129–54.

Kaplan, Carla, "Introduction: Nella Larsen's Erotics of Race," in *Passing*, Norton Critical Edition, edited by Carla Kaplan, W. W. Norton, 2007, pp. ix–xxvii.

Larsen, Nella, *Passing*, Penguin Books, 2003.

Larson, Charles R., "Nella Larsen: Voice of the Harlem Renaissance," in *The World and I*, Vol. 15, No. 2, February 2000, p. 293.

Madigan, Mark J., "From Miscegenation and 'The Dicta of Race and Class': The Rhinelander Case and Nella Larsen's *Passing*," in *Passing*, edited by Carla Kaplan, W. W. Norton, 2007, pp. 387–93.

McDowell, Deborah E., "Black Female Sexuality in *Passing*," in *Passing*, edited by Carla Kaplan, W. W. Norton, 2007, pp. 363–79.

Sullivan, Neil, "Nella Larsen's *Passing* and the Fading Subject," in *African American Review*, Vol.

32, No. 3, Fall 1998, pp. 373–86.

Thaggert, Miriam, "Racial Etiquette: Nella Larsen's *Passing* and the Rhinelander Case," in *Passing*, edited by Carla Kaplan, W. W. Norton, 2007, pp. 507–32.

Toth, Josh, "Deauthenticating Community: The Passing Intrusion of Clare Kendry in Nella Larsen's *Passing*," in *MELUS*, Vol. 33, No. 1, Spring 2008, pp. 55–73.

Wormser, Richard, "The Harlem Renaissance (1917–1935)," PBS website, https://www.pbs.org/wnet/jimcrow/stories_events_ha (accessed July 20, 2017).

Further Reading

Bennett, Juda, *The Passing Figure: Racial Confusion in Modern American Literature*, Peter Lang, 1996.

> This history of the Harlem Renaissance examines how artists, writers, critics, scholars, and readers formulated race in 1920s America, when the boundaries separating African Americans and whites were at once more severe and yet more easily transgressed than ever before.

Larsen, Nella, *The Short Fiction of Nella Larsen*, Wilder Publications, 2010.

> This collection includes three of Larsen's published short stories: "Freedom," "Wrong Man," and "Sanctuary," Larsen's final publication and the story for which she was accused of plagiarism. Although she convinced her editor of her innocence, her reputation never recovered from the accusation. Each of the stories displays Larsen's economic style and mastery of modernist prose.

McDowell, Deborah E., *"The Changing Same": Black Women's Literature, Criticism, and Theory*,

Indiana University Press, 1995.

McDowell's study of the most influential African American women writers in US history includes in-depth essays on the works of Larsen, Toni Morrison, Jessie Fauset, Alice Walker, Shirley Anne Williams, and more, as McDowell considers three major eras in the history of African American women writers: the Women's Era of the 1890s, the Harlem Renaissance of the 1920s, and the New Black Renaissance of the 1970s.

Sanchez, Maria C., and Linda Schlossberg, *Passing: Identity and Interpretation in Sexuality, Race, and Religion*, New York University Press, 2001.

Sanchez and Schlossberg examine various forms of passing—whether between races, religions, genders, or classes—and the various reasons for passing—whether recreational, educational, or for self-preservation or self-fulfillment—with a particular focus on the ways in which passing undermines the binary divisions of Western ideology.

Suggested Search Terms

Nella Larsen

Nella Larsen AND Passing

Harlem Renaissance

Larsen AND Passing AND sexuality

Larsen AND Passing AND race

modernist literature AND unreliable narrator

African American literature AND Passing

Alice Beatric Jones

Rachel Dolezal OR Nkechi Amare Diallo

CPSIA information can be obtained
at www.ICGtesting.com
Printed in the USA
LVHW04s0211300818
588625LV00004B/8/P